HEARNES LRC, MWSC

I MWS 00 0 150233S

DATE DUE

DATE DUE			

Missouri Western State College Library

D1113542

THE EARTH WITHOUT YOU

**POEMS
by
Franz Wright**

**Cleveland State University Poetry Center
Cleveland Poets Series No. 26**

PS
3573
.R5327
E2
1980

ACKNOWLEDGEMENTS

Thanks to the editors of the following periodicals for publishing some of these poems:

THE ANTIOCH REVIEW: "Your Last Poem," "Brussels, 1971," "The Wish," "Autumn on West Lorain Street."

BLUE BUILDINGS: "Munch's Painting of a Sick Child," "The Brother."

DURAK: "The Road," and "Orpheus, Eurydice, Hermes."

FIELD: "Thinking About Suicide," "St. Paul's Greek Orthodox Church Minneapolis 1960," "Drinking Back."

IRONWOOD: "Brugge," "Poem With No Speaker."

KAYAK: "Hand," "Cemetery."

MOONS & LION TAILES: "Morning."

THE MISSOURI REVIEW: "Sarah Bitterfield: Poem From a Woman's Dream Journal."

THE VIRGINIA QUARTERLY REVIEW: "The Visit," "View From an Institution."

"Morning," "Drinking Back," and "The Old" also appeared, thanks to David Young, in *Tapping the White Cane of Solitude*, by Franz Wright (Triskelion Press, 1976).

I would especially like to thank Larry Levis and Tom Lux for their guidance and friendship.

This book was published with the aid of a grant from the Ohio Arts Council, which is hereby gratefully acknowledged.

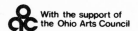
With the support of
the Ohio Arts Council

Copyright © 1980 by Franz Wright
ISBN 0-914946-23-4

CONTENTS

But a long time will have to pass before my hands can come and go
As if they were without air, without light and friends . . .

— *Supervielle*

YOUR LAST POEM

When was it
you first began to pack?
The earth was already, secretly, the earth
without you.   Because you left
your battered clothes behind.   You left
no address.   You simply left,
that's all.   And when the first star occurred
to the sky,
you opened — just a crack —
the cellar-door of the grass . . .

60 years later, it is still
dusk: it is what happens
when you return,
invisible, comatose, your empty sleeve
raised above dark waters
where the stars' reflections shine
before the stars appear.

G.T.

INITIAL

To be able to say it: rose, oak, the stars . . .
and not to be blind!
Just to be here
for one day, only
to breathe and know when you lie down
you will keep on breathing . . .
to cast a reflection —,
oh, to have hands
even if they are a little damaged,
even if the fingers
leave no prints . . .

HAND

Striking the table it seems to impose
silence on all metaphysics.
Yet touching the word *star* in braille
or switching on a lamp, the hand
is clearly the mind's glove,
its sister, its ghostly machine.
You'd hardly call what I feel pity
as I watch it
light this match:
yet it is the hand of the child
and the corpse in me —,
the sleeper's hand, buried apart
in its small grave of unconsciousness;
the hand that's been placed in handcuffs by police;
the hand I used to touch you, once;
the cold hand on my forehead . . .

SOLITUDE

You're thinking of the pilot
in his glass cockpit
40,000 feet above the street
you live on
unseen
except for the white line
traced half way across the dark sky
all at once it dawns on you
the telephone is ringing
for the first time in weeks
and with equal suddenness
it ceases
as your hand goes to lift the receiver
in the next room
so that when you return to your window
the sky has grown empty the first stars

BRUGGE

I have had a strange dream: I see a young woman wearing a white dress stretched out asleep on her back in some grass. In an immense field. The sky darkening in another century . . . The sleeper's right hand floats an inch or so above the earth, the string of a kite — too high to be seen — tied around her wrist. There is no one else in sight. I stand looking on at what seems to be a great distance; and yet the slightest movement of her lashes, the most insignificant alteration in her breathing, are as clear to me as they would be to somebody kneeling beside her and peering into her troubled, unrecognizable face . . . I don't approach her. I am in no position to bless the alone. I move in and out of their fragile world erratically and by complete accident . . . I make one more attempt to place her; but now it's like trying to detect the motion of the minute-hand, or watch yourself grow old in a mirror . . . Churchbells. The moon a mile off . . .

for Camille Park

11

THE ROAD

after a photograph by Matthew Levine

I see the one walking this road
I see the one with no home and no destination in mind
I see the one whose coat is thin whose shoes need mending
who is cold it's a very cold day
for stopping beside this dead cornfield
and basking one's face in those dark Rorschach clouds
I see the one whose lips say nothing
I see through his eyes I see the buried radiance in things
I see the one in his last clothes
I see the one who casts no shadow
on the road
who isn't there

THE VISIT

Almost always, it's just getting dark
when you come back, when you arrive
on this street;
dark
and perhaps just beginning to rain,

as it is, lightly, now.

Lightning
along the perimeter of the black cornfields past N. Professor,
and out back from the nursing home,
where they're putting people
to sleep.

Almost always, it's just getting dark
when I realize you are gone;
when you come here
and lie down beside me, without any clothes on
and without a body.

THOSE WHO COME BACK

You are one of those
who came back miraculously
whole. And yet
if someone shakes your hand,
if he welcomes you
into his home, without knowing it
he also welcomes in those who did not:
those who came back with hooks
protruding from their sleeves,
who came back in wheelchairs
and boxes . . .
They fill the house,
those who came back
with empty pant legs
or dark glasses; those who
came back with no voice; those
who come back in the night,
and ask you their name.

for Bruce Weigl

MUNCH'S PAINTING OF A SICK CHILD

In this half light, the half empty
wine glass on the bedside table
seems in contact
with dark vineyards, which go on ripening
in the first stars.

Her small skull
propped up on its pillow
might feel slightly cool to the touch
like an infant's, the delicate
continents of bone still closing . . .

So might the fingers
of her left hand
as they mingle
with those of a woman,
the mother

who's there, upright
in a chair
at her side: for the grave
has come into the bedroom,
her blanket is green.

THE OLD

Their fingernails and hair continue to grow.
The bandaged eggs of their skulls
are frequently combed by the attendants
and friends no one has told them are dead.

A few of them wander around in the hallway,
waiting to be led off to the bathroom.
And these move as if underwater, as if
they were children in big people's shoes,

exploring each thing in their own rooms
for the first time:
mirror, glasses, a vial of morphine
with a name typed microscopically on it,

impossible to make out.

Their memories tear
beside places recently stitched . . .

When I get up in the morning I'm like them
for four or five minutes: I'm anyone
frightened, hungry, somnambulistic, alone.

Wind rustles the black trees.

Then I grow young.

THINKING ABOUT SUICIDE

I know it isn't true that
after a man is buried his lips go on moving.
That graveclothes can rise to their feet
and come visit,

that they know how to
knock on both doors at once.

I refuse to board the train that carries my
coffin back and forth across America
and holds up traffic for four minutes
in the middle of the night in Kent, Ohio.

I have very little time for pilgrimages
through the cathedrals of moonlit barns
where ninety men from the eastern front are dying,
and one young man who isn't Christ, trying to heal them.

And I'd rather not have to write any more of
those foot-in-the-grave letters people
who're suffering write to cripple the fortunate.
The ones that say: I am your friend, believe me,

I'd give you the shroud off my back.

BRUSSELS, 1971

Some night
I will find myself walking
the sunlit halls of the school for the blind
I used to walk past every day
gliding by one vacant classroom
after another all at once I will stop
inside the doorway
of one where a child
in white shirt and black tie sits
alone at a desk
both hands asleep
upon the pages
of an immense book
where leaves' shadows stir

and when I wake up
I will not remember
it will still be dark
and I will lie there a long time
hearing things
the trees outside a car
starting its engine
a block away
a voice of a bird
the last stars will fade
and I will open my eyes

for Carolyn

ST. PAUL'S GREEK ORTHODOX CHURCH
MINNEAPOLIS, 1960

There are times I can still
sense the congregation
all around me, whispering
to the one who raised the dead;
the one whose own
pulse had ceased, and yet returned
from the grave.

His face above
in the high
enormously bright golden dome
of the ceiling:
the face of Christ,
so different
from the human

face of Jesus clenched
with agony,
or the beautiful Lord
of Hieronymus Bosch,
bearing the cross
in his sleep . . .
Each Sunday morning

my quiet lost mother
brought me among them there;
they were mostly old people
on canes, and some I remember
were blind: all of them dead
by now, in their Father's mansion
under the grass . . .

CEMETERY

Each name here
is a voice
in the choir
of a breath
held forever.

POEM WITH NO SPEAKER

Are you looking
for me?   Ask that crow

rowing
across the green wheat.

See those minute air bubbles
rising to the surface

at the still creek's edge —
talk to the crawdad.

Inquire
from the thin mosquito

on your wall
stinging its shadow,

this lock
of moon

lifting
the hair on your fingers.

When the heart in the cocoon
starts to beat,

when the spider
begins its secret task . . .

When the seed sends its first threads
                                creeping,

you'll have to get down on all fours

to learn my new address:
you'll have to place your skull

beside this silence
no one hears.

in memory of Frank Stanford

ORPHEUS, EURYDICE, HERMES

by Rainer Maria Rilke

a translation

This was the eerie mine of souls.
Like silent silver-ore
they veined its darkness.   Between roots
the blood that flows off into humans welled up,
looking dense as porphyry in the dark.
Otherwise, there was no red.

There were cliffs
and unreal forests.   Bridges spanning nothing
and that huge gray blind pool
suspended above its remote floor
like a stormy sky over a landscape.
And between still gentle meadows
appeared a pale strip of road.

They came along this road.

In front the slender man in the blue cloak,
mute, impatient, looking straight ahead.
Without chewing his footsteps ate up the road
in big bites; and both his hands hung
heavy and clenched by the pour of his garment
and forgot all about the light lyre
which had become like a part of his left,
rose tendrils strung in the limbs of an olive.
His mind like two minds:
meanwhile his gaze went on ahead, like a dog,
turned, and always returned to him out of the distance
to wait for him at the next bend —,
his hearing remained with him, like a scent.
At times it seemed to reach all the way back

to the movements of the two others,
who ought to be following the entire ascent.
All at once there was nothing behind him, nothing
but the echo of his own steps and the small wind
made by his cloak.   And yet
he told himself: they were coming, once;
said it out loud and heard it die away . . .
They *were* coming.   Only they were two
who moved terribly quietly.   Had he been allowed
to turn around just once (wasn't that look back
the disintegration of a whole work
that has to be accomplished first) of course he would have seen th
two dim figures walking silently behind him:

the god of journeys and secret tidings,
shining eyes inside the traveler's hood,
the slender wand held out in front of his body
and wings beating in his ankles;
and his left hand extended to: her.

This one who was loved so much that from one lyre
more mourning came than from women in mourning;
that a whole world was made out of mourning, in which
everything was present once again: forest and valley
and road and village, field, river and animal;
and that around this mourning-world, just like
around the other earth, a sun
and silent star-filled sky wheeled,
a mourning-sky with distorted constellations —;
this one who was loved so much . . .

But she walked alone holding the god's hand,
her footsteps hindered by her long graveclothes,
faltering, gentle, and without impatience.
She was inside herself, like a great hope,

and never thought of the man who walked ahead
or the road that climbed back toward life.
She was inside herself.   And her being dead
filled her like tremendous depth.
Like a fruit of its sweetness and darkness
she was full of her big death, still so new
that it hadn't been fathomed.

She found herself in a resurrected
virginity; her untouched genitals closed
like a young flower at evening;
and her hands were so weaned from marriage
that she suffered from the light
god's endlessly still guiding touch
as from too great an intimacy.

She was no longer the blond woman
who frequently appeared in the poet's songs,
no longer the fragrance and island of their wide bed
and no longer the man's to possess.

She was already loosened like long hair
and given away like the rain
and issued like huge provisions.

She was already root.

And when all at once the god stopped
her, and with pain in his voice
spoke the words: he has turned around —,
she couldn't grasp this and quietly said: who?

But far off, dark in front of the bright door
stood someone whose face
had grown unrecognizable.   He just stood and watched,

how on this strip of road through the meadow
with a heartbroken expression the god of secret tidings
silently turned, to follow the form
already starting back along the same road,
footsteps hindered by long graveclothes,
faltering, gentle, and without impatience.

SARAH BITTERFIELD:
POEM FROM A WOMAN'S
DREAM JOURNAL

As soon as you fall asleep
they hand you your own clothes,
the lamp and shovel.
Out in the backyard
you come to a mound
covered thinly with grass:
in the first shovel,
a child's tooth.
You keep on digging
then you have a whole set of them.
They're yellow
like kernels of hard corn,
they belong to a girl
with a field in her name,
she got buried here
in November
the day you were born.
How do you know
that?   You're asleep
and allowed
to know everything.

November, 1972

MORNING

A girl comes out
of the barn, holding
a lantern
like a bucket of milk

or like a lantern.
Her shadow's there.
They pump a bucket of water
and loosen their blouses,

they lead the mare out
from the field,
their thin legs
blending with the wheat.

Crack a green kernel
in your teeth.   Mist
in the fields,
along the clay road

the mare's footsteps
fill up with milk.

THE BROTHER

I'm speaking, of course, on the mirror, the shadow, the other. I'm addressing myself to the dreamer of the body: the one whose eyes open, at night, when you close your eyes. The one who leaves your fingerprints on things you touched tomorrow; whose glove is your hand, whose voice is your silence, whose sight is your . . . So: inside the darkest room of the darkest house on the darkest avenue in the darkest city, a man is reading a story to his blind identical twin. A man is shaving his blind identical twin. A man is straightening the tie of his blind identical twin. A man is feeding his blind identical twin soup with a large spoon. Now he's helping him on with his coat, they're about to take a little air. As they reach the corner they'll stop, the man will take care to cast a glance left and right before going on; while the brother stands perfectly still, upright, pale, statuesque, head bowed beneath a black, starless sky in rapt attention to the remote trill of a bird hidden in one of the nearby trees which line this particular street, empty of traffic. All of the windows are dark, as you know. No one on earth is awake.

THE VISITOR

Just hope he forgot the address:
don't answer your phone
for a week.   Turn out all the lights
in the house . . .
act like you aren't there

if some night when it's snowing
you see Franz Wright arrive
on your street with his suitcase
of sleeping pills, clutching that
black manuscript of blank pages.

for Keith

THE WISH

Yo quiero conversar con la araña.
— *Neruda*

I'm tired of listening to these
conflicting whispers
before sleep;
I'm tired of this
huge, misshapen body.
I need another: and what could be lovelier
than the wolf-spider's, with its small
hood of gray fur.
I'm told it can see in the dark;
I'm told how its children
spill from a transparent sack
it secretes, like a tear.
I'm told about its solitude,
ferocious and nocturnal . . .
I want to speak with this being.
I want it
to weave me a bridge.

AUTUMN ON WEST LORAIN STREET

Go to the window: the dead
leaves stream, soundlessly,
into W. Lorain Street,
chilling with no humans.
It is that time of your day
before Dr. Pierce's blind wife
appears below,
tapping her cane
and leading her young
daughter by the hand.   Two swans
glide across the lake's black
glass . . . the marble clouds glide
overhead, their huge reflections
glide across the water, and their shadow
darkens your address.

DRINKING BACK

From where I am
I can hear the rain on the telephone
and the voices of nuns singing
in a green church in Brugge three years ago.

I can still see the hill,
the limestone fragment of an angel,
its mouth which has healed with
the illegible names in the cemetery,

with the braillelike names of dead people.
The names of children, suicides, and the rest.
The names of people
buried with their watches running . . .

They are not sleeping, don't lie.

But it's true that once
every year of their death
it is spring.

VIEW FROM AN INSTITUTION

Thirty miles or so south of L. A.
stand two hangars, like two tombs
on the plain between
the freeway and the mountains,
remote dark swarms of army helicopters every hour
departing and arriving: I still
feel too sick even to think
we lived in their presence,
their shadows,
for nearly a year.   Oh yes, I remember
it.   And when I can't sleep
I think of huge observatories parting soundlessly
or those two domelike structures
we passed once on the coast highway,
the nuclear reactor eerily lit and crane-manipulated all night long . . .
And when I'm by myself,
this is my demented song:
welcome to the University —
it seems you're the only one registered this fall.
You'll notice our nocturnal sprinkling-system.
You'll notice the library's books are all blank on the inside

for B

TO HER

It was still dark out still snowing
You were still here still asleep

When the leaves came out
Their shadows came out too

I cannot remember the summer
I cannot remember your voice

But it is still dark out still snowing
You are still here still asleep

Franz Wright was born in Vienna in the spring of 1953. His family stems from Ohio, where he currently resides after having lived in nearly every other area of the United States. He holds a bachelor's degree in English Literature from Oberlin College, where he received an Academy of American Poets Award in 1976. He has also studied at the University of Brussels and at both the Berkeley and Irvine branches of the University of California. His other books are: *Tapping the White Cane of Solitude* (Triskelion Press); a translation of *Jarmila. Flies: 10 Prose Poems of Erica Pedretti* (Pocket Pal Press); a translation of Rilke's *The Life of Mary* (Middle Earth Books); and Herman Hesse's *Wandering*, translated in collaboration with James Wright (Farrar, Straus & Giroux).